COLOR
WITH
BRIAN CLARKE

Collages 1

"Art has been the great passion of my life:
a magnificent adventure. I hope this book
sparks your creativity and helps you
to find the joy and magic in art."

Brian Clarke

HENI Publishing, London

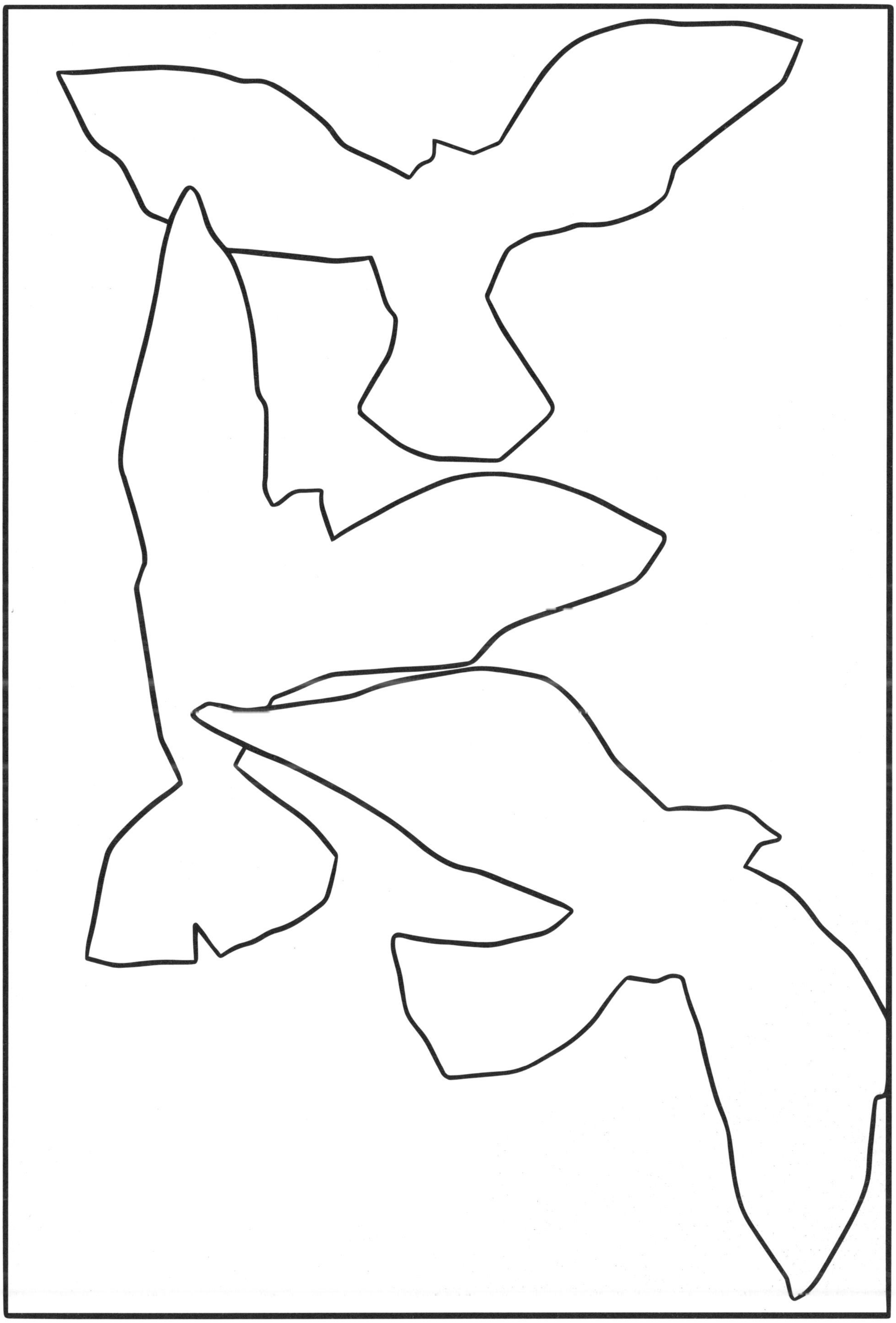

ISBN 978-1-912122-83-7

 A catalogue record for this book is available from the British Library.

Designed by Johanna Armstrong
Printed and bound in Malaysia

MIX
Paper | Supporting responsible forestry
FSC® C101773
FSC www.fsc.org